Messy Church: it's church, but not as you know it. Every month thousands of people come together to discover Jesus, including those who have never been to church before. In over 30 countries around the world, we eat, play and worship together. Expect activities, songs and prayers and an entirely new way to express your faith.

15 The Chambers, Vineyard
Abingdon OX14 3FE
brf.org.uk

Bible Reading Fellowship is a charity (233280)
and company limited by guarantee (301324),
registered in England and Wales

ISBN 978 1 80039 224 3
First published 2012
This edition published 2023
10 9 8 7 6 5 4 3 2 1 0
All rights reserved

Acknowledgements
Scripture quotations are taken from The Holy Bible, New International Version
(Anglicised edition) copyright © 1979, 1984, 2011 by Biblica. Used by permission of
Hodder & Stoughton Publishers, a Hachette UK company. All rights reserved. 'NIV'
is a registered trademark of Biblica. UK trademark number 1448790.

Every effort has been made to trace and contact copyright owners for material
used in this resource. We apologise for any inadvertent omissions or errors, and
would ask those concerned to contact us so that full acknowledgement can be
made in the future.

A catalogue record for this book is available from the British Library

Printed and bound by CPI Group (UK) Ltd, Croydon CR0 4YY

STARTING YOUR MESSY CHURCH

LUCY MOORE, JANE LEADBETTER
AND AIKE KENNETT-BROWN

For Lesley Baker and Denise Williams, two friends who started the first Messy Church, who have stuck with it right from the beginning, who have thrown ideas into (and, mercifully, out of) more planning meetings than any of us can remember and who have helped our Messy Church become what God wants it to be through their tireless love, faith, wisdom and hope.
Lucy Moore

For Sandra McCann and Christine Eyre at L19: Messy Church for their creativity and vision for the local community, and for the best bacon butties ever!
Jane Leadbetter

For Lucy Moore, who pioneered and championed Messy Church for 18 years, both nationally and internationally. We give thanks for your God-given creativity and inspiration that has enabled others to be bold and brave and experiment with a messier way of being church together.

For Jane Leadbetter, now retired from the BRF Messy Church team, but still continues to lead L19: Messy Church once a month. We give thanks for your passionate care of the environment and for starting us on the Messy Church Goes Wild adventure.
Aike Kennett-Brown

About the editor

Aike Kennett-Brown took over as BRF Messy Church ministry lead in 2022. She leads the BRF Messy Church team as they seek to support the Messy Church network both nationally and internationally, through writing, reflecting, speaking, developing resources and championing best practice, so the work of Messy Church can continue to transform lives. Aike has been involved with Messy Church since 2010 and has held both local and regional roles. She is currently involved with a Messy Church Goes Wild that meets near the O2 Arena, Greenwich.

THANKS TO ALL MESSY CHURCH LEADERS
WHO HAVE SHARED THEIR ADVICE
AND OPINIONS THROUGHOUT THIS BOOK

Contents

Introduction

If you're wondering about starting a Messy Church, this book is for you. It's short, punchy and aimed at those who might not have time to read the longer Messy Church books. It gets the basics across quickly and will give you a good idea of whether or not Messy Church is for you. It sets out clearly just what you'll need to consider and will also help you avoid some of the pitfalls other teams have encountered on their Messy Church journeys.

This book complements the online training provided by the BRF Messy Church team. Combined with the downloadable material on the Messy Church website (**messychurch.org.uk**), you should have all the help you need to get going with a Messy Church in your community, but don't forget that even more help will come from other people. Your neighbouring Messy Churches will be delighted to cheer you on and share their experiences. If you are in the UK, we have support teams who can help you with different aspects of your Messy Church, whether starting, restarting, running or developing your Messy Church. You can contact the support teams and the BRF Messy Church team via the website, so you need never be alone with a problem to solve or a wonderful story that you simply have to share with someone.

God has graciously and inexplicably chosen to work through many Messy Churches, drawing together teams of Christians who have suddenly found the opportunity through it to share God's story and their own story of faith in a non-threatening way, and drawing in families with no church connection to show them how warm, welcoming, relevant and fun a church can be. This may be for you too. Our prayer is that every Messy Church will be an opportunity for congregations and teams to meet Father, Son and Holy Spirit, and be a place where the kingdom of heaven has the space to grow within individuals and families to the glory of God and for the healing and wholeness of the local community.

Lucy Moore and Jane Leadbetter

Messy Church: the bigger picture

Before you leap into a morass of glue and spaghetti, ask yourself a question:

WHY ARE YOU THINKING ABOUT STARTING A MESSY CHURCH?

There may be any number of honest answers, but what matters is that you want to help people of all ages, abilities and backgrounds meet Jesus. With that in place you can't go far wrong, whatever you do.

I LOVE THE IDEA OF MESSY CHURCH. THIS IS WHAT WE NEED. I SUPPOSE WE JUST NEED TO GET ON WITH IT

Possibly good reasons for starting a Messy Church

- We want to make disciples.

- People in our area who don't belong to church might like coming to a Messy Church or a Messy Church Goes Wild.

- We want to share the love of God in Jesus in a way that's as accessible as possible to families.

- We believe that the best way for people of all ages to come closer to God is by journeying together.

- We want to share Jesus more than we want to share our particular denominational traditions.

- We want to model who Jesus is to all.

- We believe God is in Messy Church and we want to follow where he leads.

- We think Jesus is the person to give people in our community life in all its fullness.

- And many more. (In fact, many more good reasons than bad ones, we find, as we hear people getting excited at Messy Church training events. Which is reassuring.)

Possibly less good reasons for starting a Messy Church

- The church up the road is running a Messy Church, so we need to or we'll get left out.

- The minister says we need one.

- We need younger people in our church to do the jobs we used to do when we were young.

- We want to revamp our Sunday congregation.

- We want to get together for a nice sociable time with knitting and paint.

- It sounds fun.

- We're bored with sermons and want a change.

- I have a stationery fetish that I can indulge shamelessly.

A TEAM NEEDS TO BE PREPARED TO WORK HARD IN ORDER FOR IT TO BE SUCCESSFUL

Running a Messy Church is hard work, tiring and relentless, may make you vulnerable to deep disappointment and hurt, and may bring you into conflict with people who don't get it or who take you for a ride. (Sounds like the experience of Jesus already.) It will bring you into a greater intimacy with heaps of raw sausages than you really want. It will make you search your soul for answers to questions you've never thought about or cared about before. It will send you into a panic about your own Christian journey and how you articulate and live out that story. And it will be exhilarating, eye-opening, moving, radical and might/will/should change the way you look at Christ and God's church. We thoroughly recommend it.

All this is to say that starting a Messy Church is about involving you and your team and community in something bigger than 'a little kraft klub for the kiddies'. You are being a pioneer, taking on the role of a church leader, whether you're ordained or not: this is serious stuff and not to be undertaken lightly or without due reverence, as the Marriage Service says. But it's also a huge amount of fun and adventure: just save yourselves a lot of grief by deciding right from the start that you are all in the business of making disciples. The way you go about making disciples may involve horrifying amounts of icing sugar and junk modelling, but it's always there; this priority will keep you all going through the hard times: we're here to make disciples, not to try to get people to come to our church service or to give them a Nice Time. It's like an artist imagining the whole picture in her head before she knuckles down and starts painting in the detail of the clouds in the top left-hand corner: she knows in the broadest terms what the big picture will be, even if it changes hugely in the process. Messy Church, like other forms of church, traditional or new, is ultimately about making disciples.

For this to happen, the 'A Voyage of Discovery' research report published in 2021 (available on the website) recommended that a Messy Church needs to:

- Decide to be a community of reflective practice.

- Decide to notice God at work.

- Decide to be church all month.

- Decide to value quality as well as quantity.

- Decide to make Messy Church a priority, to make it a deeper, richer experience.

- Decide to journey together and be deliberately intergenerational and hospitable to others who are different.

- Decide to be disciples and to make disciples.

DON'T BE AFRAID! PRAY ABOUT IT AND GO FOR IT

What Messy Church is and isn't

All this is explored in depth in *Messy Church*, the first book. But as you have taken the trouble to buy this one, here's a brief recap: it's a way of being church based on the values of being Christ-centred, for all ages, that involves creativity, celebration and hospitality. Messy Churches come in different shapes and sizes. Most gather monthly at a time and place that suits people who don't already belong to church and usually looks something like this: welcome, activity time, celebration or 'overt' worship, meal. More recently, you might discover a Messy Church Goes Wild that meets outside, helping people encounter God through nature, encouraging us to be more eco-aware in all we do.

It's not a way of attracting more people to your existing Sunday services, though this might happen.

It's a church for people at all stages of their faith journey and of any age, a congregation that is as valuable and worthy of investment as any of your other congregations.

In the words of Archbishop Justin Welby: 'This is not church for children, it's church for church. It's church for everyone.'

Children are an integral part of the congregation and are both models of discipleship and disciples themselves, as are the adults who play the same dual roles. You'll see an experienced Christian learning from a less experienced one and vice versa; a child teaching an adult; sometimes one family learns from another en masse; sometimes the Christian community demonstrates how to live for Jesus to those who don't yet know him; sometimes a parent or carer teaches a child something.

If discipleship needs a mixture of formal learning, informal learning and social learning, Messy Church has elements of all three as it (formally) explores the Bible through activities and story, provides opportunities for informal conversation and observation, and encourages all sorts of levels of social learning both at the gathered Messy Church and in encouragement to take that learned faith back into the home during the rest of the month. Of the three sorts of learning, it is stronger on the social and informal ways of learning.

A GOOD RELATIONSHIP WITH THE LOCAL SCHOOL(S) HELPS AS THEY CAN ADVERTISE THROUGH FLYER DISTRIBUTION OR NEWSLETTERS. PERHAPS A MESSY CHURCH LEADER COULD TALK ABOUT MESSY CHURCH IN ASSEMBLY? COULD YOU MEET IN THE SCHOOL BUILDING AT THE END OF THE SCHOOL DAY?

How it all began

Messy Church began in 2004 at the Anglican church of St Wilfrid's in Cowplain, a suburb of Portsmouth. As Lucy Moore was on the core team of this first Messy Church and was also working for BRF's ministry among children, BRF was the logical place to base the wider ministry of Messy Church as it developed in training, website and resources, giving the movement the backing of a larger infrastructure than St Wilf's could have provided.

BE PATIENT WITH EACH OTHER — YOU ALL HAVE THE SAME OBJECTIVE BUT MAY COME AT IT FROM DIFFERENT BACKGROUNDS

Messy Church values

Messy Church can be adapted to many different contexts; however, the common theme between different expressions of Messy Church is the Messy Church values: Christ-centred, for all ages, creativity, celebration and hospitality. If you feel able to sign up to these values, we encourage you to join the Messy Church network by registering your Messy Church on the Messy Church directory (**messychurch.org.uk/messy-churches**), so that others can find you.

Christ-centred means that Jesus is at the heart of everything we do and the way we do it. This involves encountering Christ as we plan and prepare. It includes hearing about Jesus and talking about him as we take part in the different elements of Messy Church, using our common interest in craft, science or nature as a springboard to bring people closer to Jesus Christ. Messy Church tries to be a gathering of people whose identity is, or might one day grow into being, in Christ.

All-age is shorthand for being church for everybody, welcoming all ages, abilities, learning preferences, backgrounds, levels of interest in God, spiritual styles. Having everyone present, knocking up against each other in the same room and doing the same activities is important to us. Messy Church is an opportunity to enjoy the life, liveliness, loving care and purpose of the family of God at all stages of life.

Creativity is about reflecting who God is as creator of new things and re-creator of people and communities who are broken. It comes across most strongly in the activity time but bubbles up in the imaginative approach to dealing with problems and opportunities, and being flexible to change anything inessential to meet the needs of a particular context, season or person. Awe and wonder is part of creativity, whether it's learning how to use scissors for the first time, or marvelling at God's creation whilst hunting for minibeasts.

Hospitality runs through every Messy Church like a golden thread, mirroring the hospitality of Jesus in the way he welcomed those on the edges of society, both young and old, providing food for the hungry and enjoying food provided by others. It means shaping what we do around the needs of those who are marginalised, and being ready to be changed by them. It's about welcome and food and grace and giving.

Celebration is about the joy of being a child of God and a member of this marvellous body we call the church. It's about saying yes, there is a huge amount to celebrate in our faith life, even if the world around us is falling apart. It's also about celebrating in the sense of 'marking' or 'recognising as significant' each person, each family, the church community and the God we serve.

Why the shape?

With the Messy Church values embedded in all you do, the shape of Messy Church can flex around your context, your facilities and the time of day you meet. We suggest it contains the following elements:

The welcome

The welcome time comes from an understanding that the people who come to a Messy Church often don't come into a church easily; they need an encouraging warm welcome. An afterschool Messy Church may need a longer welcome time than a weekend one, as arrivals from different schools mean a very staggered starting time, whereas at the weekend, most people can arrange to arrive at around the same time. An unstructured time of conversation, colouring, chilling, chatting with drinks and snacks can be a relief after a structured day.

The activities

The activities give an hour for leisurely and unhurried experimentation and enjoyment of the various activities. Activities could include sport, craft or science activities, cooking or exploring the natural world. The number of activities varies but may be between four and ten, enough to allow plenty to fill the time but not so many that people feel overwhelmed by choice. When meeting outdoors, we find activities take longer and fewer are required. They are all themed around the Bible theme of the day and may well come at the subject tangentially or obliquely (but are no less valuable for that). There is a variety of activities to appeal to both genders and all ages and learning styles.

The celebration

Whilst we consider everything in Messy Church, including the welcome, activities and meal, part of the act of worship, the celebration time makes the theme overt and articulates some of the learning, placing it in the context of worship rather than cerebral knowledge alone. It is a celebration of God, of the redeeming work of Jesus, of our lives and identity in his story, of our community life and identity as well as our family and individual lives. It could involve: finding out what people have discovered during the activities; storytelling using video clips or a drama to highlight the Bible story; songs that relate to the theme;

questions to help you wonder; a short testimony of how God is at work today; individual and corporate prayers; other languages, such as BSL or Makaton, depending on your community. Each element should relate to the theme to bring it home in a variety of ways. It's best to keep this short, simple and as interactive as possible. We encourage adult leaders to work alongside young people to lead the celebration time.

The meal time

The meal feeds body and soul as the congregation sits around tables or picnic rugs as equals and break bread (or pasta or jacket potatoes) together in a non-verbal expression of the feast of the kingdom of heaven, where all are accepted and everyone belongs without a need to earn their place or fight for recognition and status.

Each of these elements of Messy Church provides opportunities to build relationships and show who God is in words and actions.

IT WILL TAKE TIME. DON'T EXPECT TO SHARE THIS ONE MEETING AND HAVE IT ALL RUNNING A MONTH LATER. IT MAY TAKE SIX MONTHS

What is Messy Church Goes Wild?

Messy Church Goes Wild is the movement within Messy Church which aims to encourage Messy Churches to meet God outdoors, love the natural world, experience a sense of awe and wonder there, and to be more eco-aware in all we do, both inside and out, as gathered and dispersed church, for the good of the planet.

Connecting with the five core values of being Christ-centred, for all ages, creativity, hospitality and celebration, Messy Church Goes Wild has developed out of a growing awareness of environmental issues and the realisation that the church has a part to play in the care of God's creation. Whether Messy Church meets indoors or outdoors, we can all play our part to reduce, reuse and recycle our waste and become more eco-aware in our activities, both at home and at Messy Church.

It also offers the opportunity to encounter God through nature. Children often experience awe and wonder when exploring the natural world. If it is true of children, it may also be true of many adults. Church buildings can also be oppressive for some, so taking church outdoors is an opportunity to go out to another 'edge' and find a new group of people who have an affinity for meeting God through the glory of the natural world.

Our adventures outside were accelerated by the Covid-19 pandemic when it was safer to meet outdoors in the fresh air.

The shape of Messy Church Goes Wild

To support this movement, the resource, *Messy Adventures*, provides twelve units of materials, including fun activities with a strong scientific focus, questions to discuss, 'Big thinking' provided by scientific experts and suggestions for creative ways of responding in Christian worship with awe, wonder and celebration.

Within each unit there are materials for:

Section 1: On the move – a walk around your area, pausing at different points to play, talk, think, question, wonder and encounter God together.

Section 2: Adventure area in one spot – a session at a fixed site away from your usual meeting place. The material is deliberately unstructured to give space for the group to explore freely but with purpose.

Section 3: Activities – ideas for exploring the theme in a churchyard, garden or car park. This is most similar to an indoor Messy Church, but done outside, making use of the natural resources you find. You can pick and mix ideas between these different approaches or choose to add one or two outdoor activities to your indoor Messy Church.

At some point on your Messy Adventure, we encourage you to gather for a short celebration, with prayers, Bible story and response, and if you are comfortable with unaccompanied singing, maybe a song.

It's good to keep up the Messy Church tradition of hospitality by sharing food together, whether that's through a shared picnic, or simply toasting marshmallows over a firepit. As we seek a more sustainable approach to care for our planet, consider what to do with any waste food and rubbish disposal.

IT TAKES COMMITMENT TO
INTRODUCE OUR COMMUNITY TO JESUS

Getting your Messy Church started

Prayer

As soon as you start thinking about starting a Messy Church, begin praying and encourage others to pray too.

Wholeheartedness

Janet Tredrea from Cornwall writes of her wide experience of Messy Churches:

I can think of one (rural church) which has needed an injection of new life in which all the members can take part. The idea of Messy Church was put to the remaining members (numbers depleted recently as several left the congregation because of disillusionment and lack of vision) as a last-ditch attempt to promote the gospel to outsiders. It was stressed that everyone had to take ownership – the elderly could pray, give donations of food or money and all the able-bodied were to join the 'hands-on

team'. It worked – the Spirit was fanned back into more prominent life, team spirit is vibrant, fellowship is had every month in studying the topic of the next session and that dying church now has an active 'wing' to which the outside community is sitting up and taking notice and enthusiastically supporting. The disillusioned are back on the team and the dying church has been 'resurrected'!

This story illustrates the power of having a whole church committed to a Messy Church and the 'payback' for insisting on an all-or-nothing approach. Churches work in different ways and what was right for this church may be wrong for another, where the Messy Church might be overpowered if every member of the inherited church was committed to serving on the team.

Frequency

Most Messy Churches operate monthly. This is still a considerable commitment when so many aspects of this style of church have to be pulled together for the Messy two hours. Being monthly rather than weekly has the advantage that it gives time for preparation, reflection and making changes between one month and the next. Many team members find it easier to commit to a monthly session than to a weekly one, and many Messy congregation members find the same in their busy lives. There are some brave Messy Churches that meet weekly but take a break during school holidays. Similarly, there are Messy Churches that spring up during the holiday season. What works depends on your local context, the community you are trying to reach and the availability of your team.

Remember, a key finding to make disciples in Messy Church is to consider what it means to be Messy Church all month. This might mean making space to be Messy Church in different, perhaps smaller ways in those weeks between the main gatherings. These may be opportunities to gather together with the purpose of coming closer to Jesus and to each other, but may also be about developing an attitude of mind that says, 'I am Messy Church when I'm at the toddler group/faced with a big decision/outside the school gates/walking the dog/at work' (or whatever makes up the other 30½ days of your month).

Team

Messy Church is not a solo effort ministry but requires a team. Many Messy Churches operate very well with a small core team and a larger 'turn up on the day' team. It hardly needs saying that the more envisioned and committed everyone is, the more effective your Messy Church is likely to be in its mission. This dedication might come further down the line, and you may find the team grow in excitement and commitment as they see God at work, rather than coming to the first Messy Church with all guns blazing. You may or may not want to read that leaders repeatedly say that they're glad they didn't know when they started how tiring it would be!

Volunteering has decreased in all sectors following the pandemic and so you might like to consider recruiting from within those who attend your Messy Church, developing a greater sense of ownership within the community, or changing your Messy Church model from the team 'doing this for others' to a gathering where everyone has a role. Belonging and having a purpose within the community is part of the discipleship journey towards believing. For more ideas, check our our short video 'How to build your team' at **messychurch.org.uk/resource/how-to-guides**.

Support

The minister and leadership team of the church is a crucial body to have onside. If you don't have their support, you should seriously consider whether the idea is the right way forward, or if it's going to work or have any longevity. It could provoke division and competition if it is not supported at all levels of your church.

Money

Some Messy Churches provide everything for free; some have donation buckets, QR codes to donate online or card readers available and some charge a small entrance fee. A contribution from your 'sending church' is a gesture of commitment and will ease the way as you discover what you are likely to need to budget every month. If people protest, either explain the missional aspect of what you're planning or check what the flower budget is each month.

With a spirit of being more cost-effective and eco-aware in all we do, you don't need 'posh crafts' from pre-prepared packages. Some of the most successful activities use junk or seasonal materials that can be collected for free, such as pine cones, feathers or mud.

You can build a wider supportive community beyond your Messy Church attendees by asking for donations of specific items such as empty and clean jam jars from all your congregations and church community or neighbourhood WhatsApp groups; they will be pleased their junk can be reused by someone else. Look and see what you already have around you and work with that before you buy new materials. It's always worth investigating your local scrap store or larger stores that might have ex-display or cardboard packaging they are willing to donate.

When it comes to food, opt into supermarket community schemes and ask your local supermarket for help. Vegetarian food is often cheaper than meat-based products. You might also consider a bring-and-share meal a couple of times during the year.

Space

A church building has advantages: it may be superficially rent-free, be associated with the historical Christian presence in the area, have storage space and have been prayed in for centuries. But it may be cold, dangerous, inhospitable and lack a kitchen or toilet. Schools, pubs, cafés, community and village halls, church gardens or the local park are all viable alternatives.

Work together?

Many Messy Churches work brilliantly where two or three churches have joined together to run one joint Messy Church. Some partnerships plan the session together but deliver in two different locations, pooling volunteers from local churches: is this an option for you? Perhaps you could consider forming an ecumenical partnership with your neighbouring church from a different denomination?

The wider network

If you set up your Messy Church in a vacuum relating to nobody else, you may be missing out and others cannot benefit from your experience. Joining a local, a denominational or the whole international Messy network is one step you can take to help sustain you and the team in days ahead which may be tougher if the initial pioneering spirit wears off and tiredness sets in. You can keep in touch by signing up to the newsletter, Directory on the website, or by following the BRF Messy Church Facebook, Instagram or Twitter feeds. In the UK there are support teams of experienced practitioners available to support you on your journey. We highly recommend meeting with your neighbouring Messy Church teams to pray together, share ideas and maybe plan something missional together in your local area to increase your visibility in the community.

Health and Safety

DBS CHECKS

The best thing is to talk to your safeguarding officer or the representative who deals with the safeguarding of children and vulnerable adults. It is expected that all children who attend Messy Church come with an adult (parent, carer, grandparent, family member over 18 years old). However, not every adult has to come with a child!

Each denomination and area has different rules for this form of church where children are present but are the responsibility of an adult, rather than of the church.

It is likely core team members will need to have enhanced DBS checks and attend safeguarding training. Some basic good-practice guidelines should be distributed to and discussed with all team members.

FOOD SAFETY

You may want to consider if your kitchen staff should be trained, such as with a basic food hygiene qualification.

1.   Food safety law

Food supplied, sold or provided at charity or community events must comply with food law and be safe to eat. Your responsibilities will vary depending on several factors including scale, frequency and complexity.

Practical guidance on how to comply with the law in these circumstances is provided by the Food Standards Agency on their webpages (**food.gov.uk/safety-hygiene/providing-food-at-community-and-charity-events**).

Food safety will be a more significant concern if you prepare food regularly in an organised way – for example, running a restaurant, café or other catering business; providing charitable support (e.g. for the homeless); or if you are an employer who has a restaurant or use outside caterers. In these circumstances, further guidance and resources are available (**food.gov.uk/consumer-advice/ food-safety-advice**).

2.   Basic food safety guidelines for churches

Depending on what you are doing, typical precautions could include:

- Keeping church premises clean, well maintained and in good condition if food is prepared there.

- Ensuring food preparation surfaces are in good condition, easy to clean and disinfected regularly.

- Purchasing food from reputable suppliers.

- Paying attention to any 'use-by' dates.

- Storing raw and ready-to-eat food properly.

- Making sure that food is cooked and prepared properly.

- Keeping food covered to help protect it from bacteria and prevent contamination.

- Adopting good hygiene practices when preparing food.

Please note: this list is not exhaustive.

We strongly recommend that you contact your Local Authority for specific questions concerning your context.

RISK ASSESSMENTS

The risk assessment is intended to be a useful document specific to the activity time in Messy Church. It should help a team consider any risks beforehand and make sure appropriate measures are put in place to make sure both people and property are kept safe. It isn't intended to be used by the kitchen team as cooking has its own discrete set of risks and therefore should have its own risk assessment. You can find a template on the **messychurch. org.uk** website; however, your denomination will likely have their own template.

Remember to also undertake or check out your venue's risk assessment for moving around the building or outside space.

We recommend you check your sending church's insurance policy to see what's covered, particularly if you are meeting outdoors or off-site at another venue.

TOP TIP: YOU MIGHT NOT NEED TO START FROM SCRATCH! YOUR CHURCH WILL ALREADY HAVE RISK ASSESSMENTS, SO MAYBE YOU COULD ADAPT AN EXISTING ONE.

FIRST AID

Generally, if someone is injured you may need to show that you have met your duty of care. As always, consult your denomination on the precise requirements, but these are some things you may want to think about:

- Appointing a person(s) to take charge of first aid arrangements.

- Providing a suitably stocked first aid box.

- Providing an adequate number of **qualified first aiders** for the size of the gathering.

- Providing additional training for first aiders where there are special hazards.

- Checking that the team and others know the precise location of first aid equipment and identities of nominated person(s) or first aider(s).

- Informing the emergency services of specific hazards in advance (e.g. bell tower access).

- Ensuring adequate first aid cover if your first aider is absent.

Messy admin

You can find a whole set of forms, documents and ideas for the use of those leading and planning a Messy Church session on the **messychurch.org.uk** website. As with everything, you will need to consult with your church on the denominational requirements. What we have on our website includes:

Volunteer role descriptions (part of DBS regulations) – **messychurch.org.uk/resource/role-descriptions**

Messy Church risk assessment – **messychurch.org.uk/resource/messy-church-risk-assessment**

Advice on taking photographs – **messychurch.org.uk/resource/advice-taking-photographs**

Registration forms – **messychurch.org.uk/resource/registration-form**

Messy Church activity planning grid – **messychurch.org.uk/resource/messy-church-planning-grid**

PRAY TOGETHER. PLAN TOGETHER. PLAY TOGETHER.

Checklist of starting strategies

- Listen to God.

- Listen to people outside church.

- Communicate with people in church.

The rest is detail, but it may help to…

- Pray.

- Pray some more with other people.

- Think imaginatively about your area and listen to people who don't go to church or who are on the edge of church to find out what the real needs are from their point of view. You will find helpful pointers to get you going with listening to your community on the Fresh Expressions website. Check out the six-stage framework of the Godsend App.

- Watch the 'What is Messy Church?' and 'Messy Church Goes Wild' ministry videos on the **messychurch.org. uk** website homepage, and discuss with your possible core team whether it will work for you.

- Talk to your church leaders, show them the ministry videos, listen to them and pray with them.

- Visit a Messy Church near you and ask as many questions as they have patience to answer. Ask questions of the team, the congregation and the main leaders (see suggested questions on pages 47–50).

- Pray some more and listen some more. If you are sure this is a calling from God, not a flash in the pan, the easier it will be later on if things get tough.

- Talk to lots of people in your church (especially the unlikely people) to get them engaged and possibly prepared to pray/cook/be crafty/clean up and so on. Get everyone excited! Look for people on the edge who have never been asked to help before. Ask people to do discrete jobs rather than everything.

- Plan a budget and investigate sources of funding.

- Get the go-ahead from your church leadership team.

- Check you are insured under your church's policy.

- Write a list of your aims (a suggested starting point is included on page 42) and give it to your whole team.

- Get everyone DBS checked who needs to be and be clear about best practice as regards children and vulnerable adults. Get somebody qualified with Basic Food Hygiene, a First Aider and anything else your church requires you to have qualifications-wise.

- Get together a small planning team and get praying and plotting your first Messy Church. Could you include young people in your planning team? If so, how will you make this a safe space for them?

Aims of Messy Church are...

- To provide an opportunity for people of all ages to worship together.

- To help people of all ages feel they belong in church and to each other.

- To help people have fun and be creative together.

- To introduce Jesus through hospitality, friendship, activities, storytelling and worship.

THE IMPORTANCE OF PLANNING AND PREPARATION – KEEP IT SIMPLE

Why join the Messy Church network?

'God sets the lonely in families' (Psalm 68:6).

In our discussions about long-term sustainability of fresh expressions, the need to be linked into a wider network than just the local fresh expression is proving to be hugely important a few years after starting.

You may not have the time or energy to link into any Messy Church networks when you are in the throes of starting up your own Messy Church. But it is a question to look at reasonably soon, as the benefits can be enormous.

The **messychurch.org.uk** website puts you straight through to the BRF Messy Church team for enquiries or comments or to share stories. We're very accessible and will reply as soon as we possibly can. You'll also find resources and ideas that other Messy Churches have generously contributed, plus details of the latest training available.

Here are some examples of training and resources we can offer:

- **Messy Masterclasses** are 90-minute online training sessions on various topics, including one on starting your Messy Church. They give people a chance to air reservations and hear stories of what really happens. They are advertised on the Messy Church website and are a great opportunity to meet other people at a similar stage.

- **Online Messy Meet-ups** are organised by the BRF Messy Church team to gather Messy Church core team members to swap ideas on a certain topic, ask questions, share challenges and pray for each other. They are advertised on the Messy Church website and through social media channels.

- **'How to…' short training videos** are available on the Messy Church website and YouTube channel, giving practical top tips for frequently asked questions about running a Messy Church.

- **Messy e-news**: the BRF Messy Church team sends out a monthly e-newsletter, free of charge, to anyone who signs up for it. This is a good way of staying in touch with what others are doing in Messy Church and of staying aware of new projects that may resource your own Messy Church.

- **The Messy blog** on the website offers short reflections and best practice advice, and a useful trickle of developments, encouragements and stories.

- **Follow us on social media**: search @MessyChurch-BRF on Facebook, Twitter, Pinterest and   Instagram. Support teams (in the UK) and regional coordinators (overseas) are volunteers who are passionate about Messy Church, are in close touch with BRF's Messy Church team and want to help people to do it as well as possible. The list is on the website.

- **Sign up on the Directory**: it costs nothing, nor commits you to anything. It simply provides a place where you can say 'Our Messy Church welcomes new families and visitors, and this is how you get in touch with us.' BRF finds it useful to have as many Messy Churches registered as possible as it gives us an idea of the size of the network and enables us to let you know of any developments that can resource you. We also have requests from various sources and countries asking about Messy Churches to visit, and about Messy Churches of different denominations or in different areas, and it's good for our morale to feel less than totally ignorant when we reply!

- **Visit a local Messy Church**: the Directory provides many contact details for existing Messy Churches and there may be some near you. As we've said, a very valuable step in starting up is to visit somebody else's Messy Church and learn from their experiences, both good and bad. (See the section on visiting a Messy Church on pages 47–50 for helpful details.) Once you've met the Messy Church down the road, we encourage you to stay in contact with each other to support each other locally through prayer or maybe a joint Messy mission project.

- **Bigger gatherings**: keep an eye open for the online Messtival, a morning of worship and workshops with leaders from across the nation. Every three years, the BRF Messy Church team host an in-person conference to encourage and equip your team.

- **Get Messy!** is an annual resource for Messy Church leaders, containing twelve session outlines (one per month). It is available to purchase as a download or in print, and includes short Bible reflections, activities, celebration and food suggestions, planning sheets and extra ideas. You can order it online from **brfonline.org.uk/new-get-messy.**

STICK WITH THE MESSY CHURCH BRAND. IT IS TRIED AND TESTED; DON'T FALL INTO THE TRAP OF CALLING IT SOMETHING ELSE OR TINKERING ABOUT WITH IT. EITHER DO IT OR DO SOMETHING ELSE. PLENTY OF TIME IN THE FUTURE TO MAKE ANY CHANGES NECESSARY

Questions to ask when visiting a Messy Church

Take a deep breath and enjoy the whole experience! Each Messy Church has its own wonderful characteristics but hopefully you'll find the same core values running through each one you visit. And don't panic if things are not what you expect! Sue in Wigan says: 'Two churches sent folk to see what we are doing in our Messy Church but were put off exploring further when they saw the huge numbers (190) attending. They decided they just couldn't cope with so many!'

Remember the Mess you've visited is not your church, that there are plenty of equally valid different ways of doing Messy Church and God is there in all of them.

Some suggestions for a visit

- Let the Messy Church know you are coming so someone can find time to chat with you and show you around.

- If you are travelling by car, invite others from your church to travel with you. Who knows what inspiration each person may receive!

- Try to stay for the whole time, as the Messy Church invites you to worship with them from the moment you enter until the moment you depart. It's tempting to leave before the meal, but it will give you huge insights if you stay.

- Be ready to take notes and photos to record non-people ideas like instruction sheets or welcome tables (and film only with permission, of course).

- Get contact details from people you talk to. If they are busy, you may need to follow up with questions after the visit.

Some suggestions for questions

- Why did you start a Messy Church?
- Who do you want to come to your Messy Church?
- How did you come to choose this time and day?

- How did you advertise?

- How big is your team?

- Is everyone DBS cleared?

- Is there one main coordinator or more?

- How often do you meet to plan?

- How are you funding your Messy Church?

- How much does it cost to put on one Messy Church?

- From where did you purchase your banner?

- Do you register all ages as they arrive?

- How does everyone know what to do when visiting for the first time?

- How many activities do you put on each time?

- Where did you find the activities ideas?

- Do you find the adults enjoy the activities too?

- How do the cooks know how many to cook for?

- Do you have favourite recipes to share?

- Who delivers the celebration time?

- Where do you get the songs from?

- Do you take photographs?

- Do you keep a Messy Church list of contact details?

- How do you get feedback?

- Have you given out any questionnaires?

- Do you offer anything Messy mid-month?

- What time do you get home after tidying up?

- What do you personally get out of it?

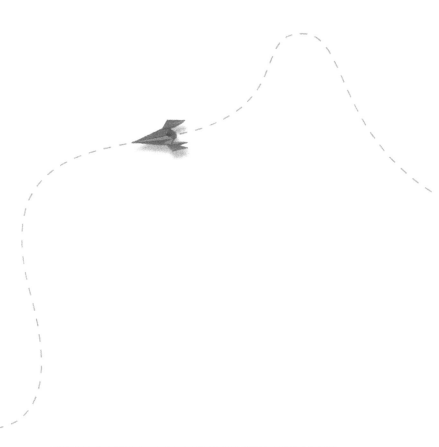

COMMUNITY TAKES TIME,
BUT IT'S EXCITING WHEN IT BEGINS TO FORM

What to expect

One glorious story tells of a Messy Church starting in a Grade 1 listed church to a congregation with no children on a Sunday. They decided that if their first session brought in 30 people they would be delighted. When numbers hit 70 and still people were coming in, the harassed kitchen team bellowed 'No more! No more! Close the doors!'

Other Messy Churches start with high numbers then find numbers dropping off after an initial boom, while others start smaller than they'd hoped and stay small for some time. There is no guarantee that your shepherd's pies will be an ample sufficiency for the three people who turn up or that you'll be praying for a miraculous multiplication of mince to feed the teeming hordes: every Messy Church is different.

When 'too many' turn up, it's worth bracing yourselves to cope without saying no to anyone for a pilot period and seeing whether numbers settle down to something manageable by the end of that time. Obviously if numbers are too high for safety, you'll have to turn people away or find an overflow venue, and if there are too many to cope with, you'll need to consider pleading with members of another local church to run one on a different day, or to join you and help out, or run a parallel one yourselves with a separate team on a different day.

Some people get excited about numbers; others see them as irrelevant. Perhaps it's worth saying that small numbers mean there is a huge opportunity to build strong intimate relationships relatively quickly, to visit effectively and to keep everyone informed; whereas large numbers mean there is a great buzz, little danger of becoming a clique and it's obvious to everyone that there is some measure of success. It's important to value quality as well as quantity – big or small, it's a win-win situation.

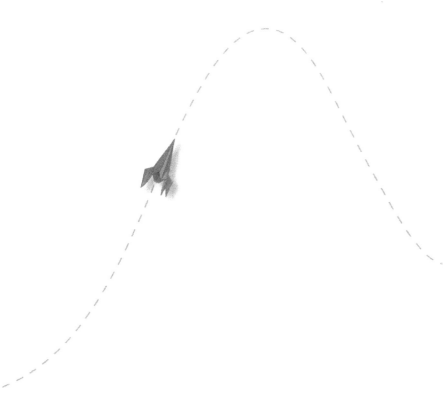

What else to expect?

Some of the following:

- Unlikely people may be your best team members.

- It may take a long time for people to 'warm up' spiritually.

- Unless you work hard at being all-age, you'll find yourselves gearing everything towards the children.

- You will get more out of it than you put into it.

- Messy problems may need Messy solutions.

- People from Sunday church may keep on expecting Messy families to come to Sunday church.

- God will work in ways you hadn't been expecting.

BE PREPARED TO BE HONEST AMONG YOUR LEADERSHIP TEAM IN ORDER TO TACKLE PROBLEMS

Organising your team

There is no one best way of organising your team. As you will have gathered, all Messy Churches are different. Here are some approaches that different churches have tried:

- Do it all yourself. This will almost inevitably result in burnout within a few months. Do not do it all yourself!

- Have a core team of two to four easy, competent, hassle-free people to work with and do all the planning and preparation with them. Let the rest of the team simply join you on the day.

- Have a leader responsible for each section of Messy Church and meet with them to get the overall picture, then leave them to organise their own areas of responsibility. You might have a welcome leader, an activities leader, a kitchen leader, a celebration leader and a discipleship leader, each of whom assembles a team of helpers. Planning meetings then simply involve the big picture rather than details.

- Treat the need for a large team as an opportunity to grow disciples and build a team from people who attend your Messy Church, who may not yet be committed Christians. View planning meetings as discipleship opportunities and train people in tasks as you go along.

- Include young people (those in the top end of primary school and older) and invite them to shape the Messy Church through the planning sessions and be shaped through their involvement. To do this well, you will have to meet at a time and place that suits the young people and have appropriate safeguarding measures in place.

- Insist that the whole of your church comes on board with some form of commitment before you can start.

- Work with another church. If you have a team but a dank, mould-ridden vault of a church, they may have a smashing building, but no one who can simultaneously manoeuvre tables, chairs and a Zimmer frame.

THE JOYS OUTWEIGH THE CHALLENGES

Sustaining your Messy Church and your team

There will be exciting positive months when everything goes well, crowds are pawing at the door asking searching questions about the place of suffering in the world and when every activity leads young and old into a deep relationship with God and with each other. And there will be months where nobody comes except your own family, half the cooks waltz off to Corfu without telling you, the heating breaks down, your own children would rather watch social media reels, the celebration team chooses a song from *Favourite Victorian Sickly Selections*, the activities appear futile and you get marbling ink all over your favourite top. Things that you can put in place before such a month to help you refrain from hiding under the duvet till it all goes away include:

- Know you are part of the network of people who want to support you (see 'Why join the Messy Church network?', page 43).

- Establish a regular training/reflection time for your team. Ask the question: Where do we notice God at work? Keep a record of 'God-moments'.

- Tell God your frustrations and ask a prayer team to commit to praying for you all every month.

- Remember that God isn't limited by mistakes, and that God's strength is made perfect in our weakness: God can and does redeem dire situations.

- Remind yourself of the bigger picture, of the way you are making disciples, and that this is slow, faithful work, not a quick fix, especially among those who have been hurt by church in the past, have rarely thought about God until now or whose family lives are remarkably messy.

- Think imaginatively about how to grow those disciples you're making. What is the next step for that one person you've noticed is interested?

IT IS EXHAUSTING AND SOMETIMES YOU WONDER WHETHER IT'S WORTH IT, BUT WHEN UNCHURCHED CHILDREN COME UP TO YOU, AT THE SCHOOL GATE OR OUT AND ABOUT, AND ASK 'WHEN'S MESSY CHURCH?' OR COME IN WITH CAKES THEY'VE MADE AT HOME TO BRING IN AND SHARE, OR THEY ENTHUSIASTICALLY JOIN IN WITH A DRAMA OR SONG, OR YOU HAVE A DEEPER CONVERSATION WITH SOMEONE THAN YOU MIGHT OTHERWISE HAVE HAD, THEN YOU KNOW IT'S WORTH ALL THE HARD WORK.

Evaluation questions after your pilot period

These are suggestions to adapt to your own situation:

Questions to ask the team

- Is our Messy Church sufficiently focused on the needs of people in our own area?

- Is our welcome effective?

- Do we provide activities for all ages and all learning styles?

- Do the activities provide links to the theme?

- Is the celebration accessible and relevant to all ages and learning abilities?

- Do we provide opportunities to meet Jesus in every stage of Messy Church?

- Is the team confident to share God's story and their own story?

- Is anyone in the team finding Messy Church too heavy a burden?

- Is everyone safe?

- Are we making disciples?

Questions to ask the congregation

(Perhaps with smiley, sad or neutral faces to circle, and space to add comments.)

- How welcome does everyone in your family or group feel?

- How do you all find the activities?

- How do you all find the celebration?

- How do you all find the meal?

- How accessible is the venue?

- How is the time and day for you?

THE MESSY CHURCH BOOKS, GET MESSY! AND MESSY ADVENTURES SESSIONS ARE EXCELLENT RESOURCES THAT WILL HELP YOU GET STARTED AND GIVE YOU MASSES OF MATERIAL FOR MANY YEARS TO COME

Be encouraged

God is doing something exciting through people like you. An email we received thanked us for what we're doing and added, 'Messy Church is changing the landscape of outreach and worship in big, big ways.' We don't know where this Messy journey will take us, but we do know that the more prayer, discernment and integrity goes into starting and sustaining Messy Churches, the more chance we have of catching the wind of the Spirit for our communities in this generation.

Enabling all ages to grow in faith

Anna Chaplaincy
Living Faith
Messy Church
Parenting for Faith

BRF is a Christian charity that resources individuals and churches. Our vision is to enable people of all ages to grow in faith and understanding of the Bible and to see more people equipped to exercise their gifts in leadership and ministry.

To find out more about our work, visit

brf.org.uk

Each issue contains twelve session outlines for Messy Churches, running through the year from September to August. Everything you need to run your Messy Church, including activity photos, mealtime cards, social action ideas and templates, all downloadable from the Messy Church website. With an introduction by Aike Kennett-Brown.

Get Messy! Volume 1 – Intergenerational discipleship

The essential magazine for Messy Church leaders

978 1 80039 180 2 £14.99 (Or subscribe and save, or buy individual sessions at £1.99 each)

brfonline.org.uk

Messy Church Goes Wild is the movement within Messy Church which aims to encourage Messy Churches to meet God outdoors, love the natural world, experience a sense of awe and wonder there and be more eco-aware in all we do, both inside and out, as gathered and dispersed church, for the good of the planet. Edited by Messy Church founder Lucy Moore, this unique collection of wisdom and practical materials covers a range of topics from caring for animals and birds through living as an eco-friendly household to greening up your Messy Church activities and running an online session on Jesus in the wilderness.

Messy Church Goes Wild
Caring for the world we live in
Edited by Lucy Moore
978 1 80039 009 6 £12.99

brfonline.org.uk

Twelve sessions for Messy Churches to do outdoors, created by a Messy Church Goes Wild writer team, enhanced by additions from scientists, and piloted in urban and rural Messy Churches.

Messy Adventures
Twelve outdoor sessions for Messy Churches (with lots of science)
Edited by Lucy Moore, Dave Gregory, Cate Williams and Jane Butler
978 1 80039 149 9 £12.99

brfonline.org.uk